HEALTHY ADAPTOGEN HERBS FOR BEGINNERS

DR. PENNY WATSON

Copyright © 2023 by Dr. Penny Watson

TABLE OF CONTENTS

INTRODUCTION

In a quiet village nestled at the foot of towering mountains, there lived a woman named Elara. She was known for her boundless energy and unwavering determination, but recently, life had thrown her a curveball.

A demanding job, family responsibilities, and the fast-paced world around her had left Elara feeling drained, anxious, and struggling to find balance. One day, as she wandered through the village market, she stumbled upon an old herbalist's stall.

The herbalist, a wise old woman named Seraphina, noticed the weariness in Elara's eyes and struck up a conversation. Seraphina shared stories of adaptogen herbs, powerful botanicals that were believed to help the body adapt to stress, restore balance, and boost overall well-being. Intrigued by the idea, Elara decided to give these adaptogens a try.

She began incorporating herbs like Ashwagandha, Rhodiola, and Holy Basil into her daily routine. At first, she didn't notice any significant changes, but as the weeks went by, subtle shifts began to occur. She found herself better able to handle her workload, her sleep improved, and her anxiety began to ebb away.

As the months passed, Elara's transformation became more evident. She radiated vitality, her smile returned, and her enthusiasm for life was contagious. Friends and family marveled at the change in her, and she happily shared the secret of her newfound well-being – adaptogen herbs.

Elara's story spread throughout the village, and soon, more and more people sought out Seraphina's herbs. Farmers, traders, parents, and students, all found solace in these natural remedies. The village began to thrive as stress levels dropped, relationships flourished, and a sense of community deepened.

Elara herself became an advocate for holistic well-being. She started gatherings where villagers could learn about herbs, share their stories, and support one another. Seraphina's stall grew busier, and the wisdom of adaptogens traveled beyond the village borders. Word reached the neighboring towns, and people from far and wide journeyed to learn from Elara's experience. The healing power of adaptogens became a beacon of hope in a world that often felt overwhelming. Elara's story became a legend, a reminder that even in the face of life's challenges, there was a way to find balance and healing through the gifts of nature.

And so, the story of Elara and her transformation through adaptogen herbs continued to inspire countless lives, weaving a tale of resilience, healing, and the remarkable ability of the human spirit to adapt and thrive.

WHAT ARE ADAPTOGENS?

Adaptogens are a class of natural substances, often found in certain herbs and plants, that are believed to help the body adapt to various forms of stress and maintain balance. These stressors can be physical, emotional, or environmental in nature.

Adaptogens are thought to work by regulating the body's stress response system, which includes the adrenal glands and the production of stress hormones like cortisol. Adaptogen herbs are specific types of plants that contain these adaptogenic compounds. They have been used for centuries in traditional medicine systems, particularly in Ayurveda and Traditional Chinese Medicine. Some well-known adaptogen herbs include:

Ashwagandha (Withania somnifera): Commonly used in Ayurveda, ashwagandha is believed to help reduce stress, promote relaxation, and improve overall well-being. It's often used to support adrenal health and cognitive function.

Rhodiola (Rhodiola rosea): Originating from Siberia, Rhodiola is thought to increase the body's resistance to various stressors and improve physical and mental performance. It's often used by athletes and individuals seeking enhanced endurance.

Holy Basil (Ocimum sanctum or Ocimum tenuiflorum): Also known as Tulsi, holy basil is revered in Ayurveda for its calming effects and potential to support immune system function. It's used to manage stress and promote mental clarity.

Eleuthero (Eleutherococcus senticosus): Also called Siberian ginseng, eleuthero is believed to increase energy levels, enhance resilience to stress, and improve overall vitality.

Schisandra (Schisandra chinensis): Used in Traditional Chinese Medicine, schisandra is thought to have a broad range of adaptogenic effects, including supporting mental clarity, reducing fatigue, and enhancing endurance.

CHAPTER ONE

Benefits of Adaptogen Herbs:

Stress Reduction: Adaptogens are often associated with reducing the body's response to stress. They may help lower cortisol levels, which are elevated during times of stress, leading to a more balanced and calmer state.

Energy and Vitality: Adaptogens are believed to increase energy levels and combat fatigue. They may help improve overall endurance and physical performance.

Cognitive Function: Some adaptogens are thought to enhance mental clarity, focus, and cognitive function, making them useful for managing mental fatigue and improving concentration.

Immune Support: Certain adaptogens, like holy basil and astragalus, are believed to have immune-boosting properties that help the body defend against infections and illnesses.

Hormonal Balance: Adaptogens may help regulate hormones and support the endocrine system, which can be particularly beneficial for women dealing with hormonal imbalances.

Anxiety and Mood: Some adaptogens have calming effects that can help reduce anxiety, improve mood, and promote a sense of well-being.

It's important to note that while there is a growing body of scientific research supporting the potential benefits of adaptogens, more studies are needed to fully understand their mechanisms of action and effectiveness. If you're considering incorporating adaptogen herbs into your routine, it's recommended to consult with a healthcare professional, especially if you have any pre-existing health conditions or are taking medications.

HOW TO ADD ADAPTOGENS TO YOUR DIET

Adding adaptogens to your diet can be a great way to potentially experience their benefits. Here's how you can incorporate adaptogen herbs into your daily routine:

Consult a Healthcare Professional: Before adding any new supplements or herbs to your diet, it's important to consult with a healthcare professional, especially if you have existing health conditions, are pregnant or breastfeeding, or are taking medications.

Choose Quality Sources: Purchase adaptogen herbs from reputable sources to ensure you're getting high-quality, organic products without additives or contaminants.

Start Slowly: When incorporating adaptogens into your routine, start with a small amount and gradually increase the dosage as your body gets accustomed to them.

Consider Form and Preparation:

Powders: Many adaptogens are available in powdered form. You can add these powders to smoothies, teas, coffees, or even sprinkle them on top of yogurt or oatmeal.

Capsules or Tablets: If you prefer a more convenient option, adaptogen supplements in capsule or tablet form are available. Follow the recommended dosage on the packaging.

Tinctures: Tinctures are liquid extracts of herbs. They can be added to water, juice, or other beverages.

Teas: Some adaptogens are available as loose herbs or tea bags. You can steep these herbs in hot water to make a soothing tea.

Create Recipes:

Smoothies: Blend adaptogen powders with fruits, vegetables, and liquids to make nutrient-rich smoothies.

Lattes: Mix adaptogen powders into milk (dairy or plant-based) for a warm or iced latte.

Baked Goods: Incorporate adaptogen powders into recipes for muffins, energy bars, or other baked goods.

Salads: Sprinkle powdered adaptogens onto salads for an extra health boost.

Pair with Other Ingredients: Some adaptogens have strong flavors, so consider pairing them with ingredients that complement their taste. For instance, cacao or honey can help balance out the earthy flavor of certain adaptogens.

Rotate Adaptogens: To avoid building up a tolerance, it's a good idea to rotate the adaptogens you use. This means using different adaptogens on different days or weeks.

Be Patient: Adaptogens may take some time to show noticeable effects. Consistency is key. Give your body several weeks to adapt and respond.

Observe Your Body: Pay attention to how your body responds to the adaptogens. If you experience any negative side effects or discomfort, discontinue use and consult a healthcare professional.

Stay Hydrated: As you incorporate adaptogens into your diet, make sure to stay well-hydrated by drinking plenty of water.

Remember that individual responses to adaptogens can vary, so what works well for one person might not work the same way for another. It's also important to maintain a balanced and healthy diet alongside incorporating adaptogens for optimal well-being.

SIDE EFFECTS OF ADAPTOGENS

Adaptogens are generally considered safe for most people when used appropriately. However, like any supplements or herbs, there can be potential side effects and interactions. Here are some considerations to keep in mind:

Individual Sensitivity: People can have varying sensitivities to different adaptogens. What works well for one person might not have the same effect on another.

Dosage: Taking excessively high doses of adaptogens can lead to adverse effects. It's important to follow recommended dosages and guidelines provided on the product packaging or by a healthcare professional.

Stomach Upset: Some adaptogens, especially in high doses, can cause digestive discomfort, including upset stomach, nausea, or diarrhea.

Stimulatory Effects: Certain adaptogens, such as Rhodiola and Ginseng, may have stimulating properties that could interfere with sleep or lead to feelings of restlessness or anxiety, especially when taken later in the day.

Interactions with Medications: Adaptogens can interact with certain medications, including blood thinners, diabetes medications, immunosuppressants, and more. It's important to consult a healthcare professional before using adaptogens if you're taking prescription medications.

Allergic Reactions: While rare, allergic reactions to adaptogens can occur. If you have known allergies to specific plants or herbs, be cautious when trying new adaptogens.

Hormonal Interactions: Some adaptogens may influence hormonal balance. If you have hormonal conditions or are on hormonal medications, consult a healthcare professional before using adaptogens.

Pregnancy and Breastfeeding: Pregnant and breastfeeding women should exercise caution when using adaptogens. Some adaptogens have not been thoroughly studied in these populations, so it's best to consult a healthcare provider before use.

Autoimmune Conditions: Individuals with autoimmune conditions should be cautious with adaptogens, as some may stimulate the immune system, potentially exacerbating autoimmune responses.

Long-Term Use: The long-term effects of consistent and prolonged use of certain adaptogens are not well understood. It's advisable not to use adaptogens continuously without breaks.

Tolerance: Regular use of adaptogens can lead to reduced responsiveness over time. To avoid this, consider rotating adaptogens or taking breaks from their use.

Quality and Source: Using high-quality, reputable adaptogen products is essential to minimize the risk of contaminants or adulteration.

To safely incorporate adaptogens into your routine:

- Consult a healthcare professional before starting to use adaptogens, especially if you have any pre-existing health conditions or are on medications.
- Start with the lowest recommended dose and observe how your body responds.
- Keep track of any changes you experience, positive or negative, and adjust your usage accordingly.
- If you experience any adverse effects, discontinue use and consult a healthcare professional.

Remember that adaptogens are just one component of a balanced and healthy lifestyle. Maintaining a nutritious diet, regular exercise, adequate sleep, and stress management practices are all important for overall well-being.

CHAPTER TWO

AMAZING ADAPTOGENIC HERBS FOR ADRENAL FATIGUE

If you feel run-down and unfocused, you may be suffering from adrenal fatigue. Adaptogenic herbs may be able to help.

Whether it's a stressful day at work, a challenging interaction with a loved one, or just the go-go-go cadence of life, we all experience moments that demand a lot of our mental, emotional, and physical energy. When this happens, our adrenal glands take a hard hit and we can feel generally off.

Here, we discuss the science and symptoms of adrenal fatigue and how adaptogenic herbs may be able to help restore balance to your tired body.

What is Adrenal Fatigue?

The adrenal glands are true multitaskers of the human body. They influence your stress response, immune health, sleep patterns, and even your mood.

These small but powerful glands produce hormones that naturally assist in maintaining functions ranging from blood pressure and cardiovascular activity to blood sugar levels and metabolism.

Because the adrenal glands are absolutely vital to well-being, we like to refer to them as the unsung heroes of the endocrine system.

When your adrenal glands are operating at 100%, you'll feel a sense of mental clarity that can help you maintain alertness throughout the day.

When your adrenal glands are fatigued, however, you'll feel physically run down with low energy levels, a weakened immune system, and an inability to adapt to stress.

Optimizing adrenal gland function is essential to combating stress and living a more balanced life. Adaptogenic herbs like those found in Gaia Herbs Everyday Adaptogen help by supporting the adrenal glands and promoting stress relief and equilibrium of mind, body, and spirit.

Adaptogenic Herbs and Adrenal Fatigue

Adaptogenic herbs are a healthy addition to your balanced diet and can help restore balance in a variety of ways.

Let's discuss how these herbs help to reduce adrenal fatigue specifically.

When you experience stress — be it physical or mental — your body begins a process called general adaptation syndrome (or GAS for short). General adaptation syndrome progresses through three stages:

1. Alarm

2. Resistance

3. Exhaustion

We'll look at each stage in a bit more detail and see how adaptogenic herbs can help.

GENERAL ADAPTATION SYNDROME

Alarm Phase

The alarm phase refers to the initial symptoms your body experiences when under stress, such as:

• Heightened senses

• Increased pulse rate

• Elevated blood pressure

• Agitation

• Sweating

During the alarm phase, your body releases cortisol (a stress hormone) followed by a boost of adrenaline to help you deal with the problem.

The alarm phase is largely autonomic meaning it's involuntary or unconscious — so you can't do much to control it.

Though the chemical response in your body is significantly less depending on the stressor, the alarm phase of the GAS is similar to the immediate surge of adrenaline you get when you see something that frightens you.

That's not to say you'll feel the same degree of the fight-or-flight response when you experience stress, but the mechanism in your body is very similar.

So, instead of releasing a large amount of cortisol and adrenaline as it does when you're frightened, your body may only release a small amount of cortisol and adrenaline when you're stressed. As we mentioned, there's little you can do to control this part of your body's autonomic system, but you can reduce the immediate impact it has by practicing meditation, deep breathing, or mindful awareness when you feel stressed.

Resistance Phase

Shortly after the initial shock of the alarm stage, your body begins to repair itself because prolonged exposure to cortisol and adrenaline can have negative effects on your health.

At the start of the resistance phase, your endocrine system releases less cortisol and adrenaline, your heart rate slows, and your blood pressure returns to normal.

For a time, your body will remain on high alert, but if you resolve the stressful situation, your hormone levels, heart rate, and blood pressure will eventually return to their normal, pre-stress levels.

That, of course, is an ideal situation that doesn't always occur in the real world. For many of us, stressful situations continue for extended periods of time.

These might not be the fight-or-flight situations we experience when danger is present, but work, family, and life in general can put demands on us that can last for days, weeks, and even months or years.

Situations such as project deadlines, illness in the family, financial trouble, not getting along with a coworker, marital issues, and a long list of others that might not be readily resolvable can cause your body to remain on high alert longer than it was meant to.

When this happens, your body continues to secrete cortisol and adrenaline and your heart rate and blood pressure stay elevated. They might not be as high as that first initial "shock" when the stress hit, but they will be above your normal resting numbers.

Over time, your body adapts to the ongoing stress, and the prolonged presence of hormones that shouldn't be there, by becoming resistant to the cortisol and adrenaline and establishing a "new norm" for your heart rate and blood pressure.

That means that even when the stress has finally abated, your body will still function as if the stress is present. The resistance phase is characterized by the following symptoms over a period of weeks or months:

• Irritability

• Frustration

• Poor concentration

• Brain fog

If the resistance stage continues for too long, your body will enter the exhaustion phase.

Exhaustion Phase

The exhaustion phase is the direct result of too much stress for too long and is exactly what it sounds like: your body no longer has the physical, emotional, and mental strength to deal with ongoing stress.

Some individuals can handle weeks, months, or years of prolonged stress, while others can only handle a few days.

The exhaustion phase may be characterized by a feeling of hopelessness, as well as other symptoms, including:

• Fatigue

• Burnout

• Depression

• Anxiety

• Decreased stress tolerance

What's more, the physical effects of the exhaustion stage can weaken your immune system and increase your risk for stress-related illnesses.

How Adaptogenic Herbs Can Help

Adaptogenic herbs are believed to offer a range of potential benefits that can help support the body's response to stress and promote overall well-being. Here's how adaptogenic herbs can help:

Stress Reduction: Adaptogens are known for their ability to modulate the body's stress response. They can help regulate the release of stress hormones like cortisol, potentially leading to a calmer and more balanced emotional state.

Energy and Vitality: Many adaptogens are thought to enhance physical and mental energy levels, helping to combat fatigue and increase overall vitality.

They can provide a natural boost without the jittery feeling associated with stimulants like caffeine.

Cognitive Function: Some adaptogens are believed to support cognitive function by improving focus, concentration, and mental clarity. This can be especially helpful during times of mental fatigue or when facing cognitive challenges.

Immune System Support: Certain adaptogens, such as astragalus and holy basil, are believed to have immune-boosting properties. They can help the body's defenses stay strong, potentially reducing the risk of infections.

Hormonal Balance: Adaptogens like ashwagandha and maca are thought to influence hormone balance. They may support the endocrine system and help alleviate symptoms of hormonal imbalances, such as mood swings and irregular menstrual cycles.

Anxiety and Mood: Some adaptogens have calming effects that can help reduce anxiety, alleviate mood swings, and promote a sense of emotional well-being.

Physical Performance: Certain adaptogens, including Rhodiola and Eleuthero, are associated with enhanced physical performance, increased endurance, and improved recovery after physical exertion.

Adrenal Health: Adaptogens are often used to support adrenal health, helping the body cope with chronic stress and preventing the negative effects of adrenal fatigue.

Antioxidant Protection: Some adaptogens contain compounds with antioxidant properties that can help neutralize harmful free radicals in the body, supporting overall cellular health.

Sleep Quality: Certain adaptogens, like Ashwagandha and Holy Basil, may have relaxing properties that can improve sleep quality and help with insomnia.

Blood Sugar Regulation: Some adaptogens, such as Ginseng and Holy Basil, are believed to help regulate blood sugar levels and improve insulin sensitivity.

Cardiovascular Health: Certain adaptogens, like Rhodiola and Ginseng, may have cardio-protective effects by supporting healthy blood pressure and cholesterol levels.

It's important to note that while adaptogenic herbs have a long history of use in traditional medicine systems and there is a growing body of scientific research supporting their potential benefits, more studies are needed to fully understand their mechanisms of action and effectiveness.

If you're considering using adaptogens, consulting with a healthcare professional is recommended, especially if you have underlying health conditions or are taking medications.

The Best Adaptogenic Herbs for Adrenal Fatigue

In the following list, we introduce you to five of the best adaptogenic herbs for adrenal fatigue that provide daily support, help promote stress relief, and restore balance.

Ashwagandha

Known for its grounding and restorative properties, Ashwagandha supports the nervous and endocrine systems and promotes a natural sleep cycle. As a nourishing tonic, Ashwagandha can help the body adapt to stressful conditions.

Adaptogenic herbs such as Ashwagandha help nourish and restore optimal health by supporting normal mood, energy levels, and overall immune function to help you stay centered and thrive in your busy life.

Rhodiola Rosea

As an adrenal adaptogen, Siberian Rhodiola rosea supports the functioning of the adrenal glands and encourages a healthy response to stress.

Rhodiola rosea is a great adaptogenic herb for adrenal fatigue. If used regularly, Rhodiola rosea can support the body's natural resistance.

Holy basil

Holy Basil, also known as Tulsi or the incomparable one, translates to balance, which is symbolic of its most common modern use.

Holy Basil helps you respond to stress in a healthy way while nourishing the mind and elevating the spirit.

As an adaptogenic herb, Holy Basil also supports adrenal health and a state of equilibrium in the body.

Eleuthero

Eleuthero is used to support mental alertness, performance and concentration, reduce stress, and help maintain healthy energy and stamina.

In Traditional Chinese Medicine, Eleuthero root is used to invigorate qi (chi or energy), strengthen and nourish the body, and to balance vital energy.

Schisandra

Regarded as a harmonizing tonic and a popular adaptogenic herb, Schisandra berries contain a blend of five distinct flavor properties, which correspond to the five phases or Elements of Traditional Chinese Medicine: Sour (Wood), Bitter (Fire), Sweet (Earth), Acrid (Metal), and Salty (Water).

Since these five flavors work synergistically to promote overall health and vitality, Schisandra is sometimes called the "ultimate superberry."

Schisandra berries can enhance the body's natural resistance and adaptation to stressful influences, support mental endurance, and help maintain overall metabolic efficiency.

CHAPTER THREE

How to Take Adaptogenic Herbs

Supplements are the easiest and most convenient way to take an efficacious dose of adaptogenic herbs.

Our energy support products, for example, come in a variety of forms including Liquid Phyto-Caps, powders, and liquids, making it extremely easy to incorporate adaptogenic herbs into your balanced diet.

You can take our Ginseng Supreme liquid herbal supplement — which is made with an invigorating blend of adaptogenic herbs, including American Ginseng and Eleuthero, that help support energy and stamina — by administering a few drops in your mouth or by adding it to your favorite food or hot beverage.

Similarly, our Everyday Adaptogen powdered herbal supplement is a great addition to recipes or beverages. Stir it into your tea or mix it into your smoothie for a healthy dose of adaptogenic herbs anytime.

For an even easier, no-mix, ready-to-take adaptogenic boost, try Gaia Herbs Adaptogen Performance Mushrooms &

Herbs vegan capsules. If you are feeling tired or rundown, this formula contains a blend of adaptogenic herbs, including Cordyceps and Ashwagandha, that support healthy energy levels.

Be sure to follow the dosing instructions of whatever adaptogenic herb you choose and talk to an Ayurvedic practitioner for more guidance and advice.

It can also be beneficial to rotate your adaptogens every six weeks so that your body can benefit from the subtle differences among herbs.

Timing

It's also important to take your adaptogenic herbs at the right time of the day to experience the best effects.

This doesn't mean you have to time it down to the exact hour and minute.

It just means you're better off taking certain adaptogenic herbs in the morning and others in the evening.

OVERCOMING ADRENAL FATIGUE

Improving adrenal health can help you live a more balanced life. In addition to herbal supplements, there are other ways you can help support your body, including adopting a healing mindset, practicing yoga, eating a healthy, balanced diet, getting enough sleep, and taking time for yourself each day.

And remember, even small changes can lead to a big improvement in how you feel.

How the Herbs and Mushrooms Work to Relieve Stress

While there's still a lot of research to be done, Blatner says what we do know is this: "Adaptogens interact with the hypothalamic-pituitary-adrenal axis (HPA), which is our body's stress response system."

In short, she says, adaptogens can help calm the following areas: the hypothalamus (a small region in your brain), your pituitary gland (found at the base of your brain), and your adrenal glands (which are located at the top of your kidneys and produce the hormone cortisol).

Cortisol is often a buzzword when it comes to stress — it's the hormone that's released by your adrenal glands during tense times, increasing your heart rate, blood pressure, and glucose levels.

While the hormone is important for those "fight or flight moments," too-high levels of cortisol over time can lead to health issues like type 2 diabetes and Cushing's syndrome, according to the Endocrine Society's Hormone Health Network.

Meanwhile, "Adaptogens have shown promise in normalizing stress hormones, such as cortisol," says Retelny.

The big caveat is that researchers are still looking into understanding how exactly these herbs and mushrooms do this. The good news? "There's likely much more research to come in this area because stress is more common in our society and people are looking for alternatives other than prescription medicine to help cope — there's more of an interest now than ever," says Retelny.

HERB SOURCES OF ADAPTOGENS THAT SHOULD BE ON YOUR RADAR

There are several adaptogenic herbs that you might consider having at home to potentially incorporate into your daily routine.

Remember that individual preferences and needs vary, so it's a good idea to consult with a healthcare professional before introducing new herbs into your lifestyle.

Here are some well-known adaptogens you might consider:

Ashwagandha (Withania somnifera): Known for its calming and rejuvenating properties, ashwagandha may help reduce stress and promote relaxation. It's often used to support adrenal health and improve overall well-being.

Rhodiola (Rhodiola rosea): This adaptogen is associated with increased energy, improved mental clarity, and enhanced physical performance. It's commonly used by athletes and individuals looking to combat fatigue.

Holy Basil (Ocimum sanctum or Ocimum tenuiflorum): Also known as Tulsi, holy basil is revered for its stress-reducing and immune-boosting properties. It can help promote a sense of calm and overall wellness.

Eleuthero (Eleutherococcus senticosus): Often referred to as Siberian ginseng, eleuthero is believed to increase energy levels, enhance resilience to stress, and support physical endurance.

Schisandra (Schisandra chinensis): Used in Traditional Chinese Medicine, schisandra is thought to have a broad range of adaptogenic effects, including supporting mental clarity, reducing fatigue, and enhancing endurance.

Ginseng (Panax ginseng): Ginseng is one of the most well-known adaptogens. It's believed to improve physical and mental stamina, boost energy, and enhance overall well-being.

Maca (Lepidium meyenii): Maca is often used to support hormonal balance, increase energy, and enhance libido. It's also rich in vitamins and minerals.

Astragalus (Astragalus membranaceus): This adaptogen is known for its immune-boosting properties. It's believed to support overall immune system function and help the body resist infections.

Cordyceps (Cordyceps sinensis): Considered both an adaptogen and a medicinal mushroom, cordyceps is believed to improve energy, enhance exercise performance, and support lung and respiratory health.

Licorice Root (Glycyrrhiza glabra): Licorice root is often used to support adrenal health, reduce stress, and soothe the digestive system. It's important to use licorice root in moderation due to its potential effects on blood pressure and potassium levels.

Remember that these adaptogens can come in various forms, such as powders, capsules, teas, and tinctures. It's a good idea to start with one or two adaptogens and observe how your body responds before introducing more.

Also, rotate the adaptogens you use to prevent potential tolerance buildup.

Before incorporating any new herbs or supplements into your routine, it's wise to consult a healthcare professional, especially if you have underlying health conditions, are taking medications, or are pregnant or breastfeeding.

Should You Try Adaptogens for Stress Relief?

If you don't have any other health concerns, adding adaptogens to your diet may be worth a shot. We do know stress is an epidemic, and if adaptogens are a potential stress protector, and they're not going to hurt you, then why not try them?

Some people are almost immobilized by stress, and not working at their best.

It's always best to consult with your registered dietitian or doctor before you start taking any supplements.

Remember that while adaptogens may be beneficial in the long run, they probably won't solve all your stress-related woes because, nothing is really a miracle cure. You need time and proper dosage.

CHAPTER FOUR

WHY YOU NEED ADAPTOGEN HERBS AND HOW TO CHOOSE THE RIGHT ONE FOR YOU

Holy basil

People in our modern age are under a lot of pressure. And while it's only natural for the human body to release the hormone cortisol in response to stress, elevated cortisol levels cause us to live in a perpetual state of fight-or-flight.

Chronic stress can have a negative impact on our bodies, especially affecting our adrenal glands and thyroid. In addition, stress is also linked to increased risk of asthma, diabetes, depression, obesity, heart disease, Alzheimer's and gastrointestinal issues.

For thousands of years, humans have used adaptogen herbs—a group of medicinal plants known to help balance, restore, and protect the body—to combat stress, and their results are nothing short of impressive. Research shows that adaptogens can help our bodies recover from chronic stress and improve stress-related health disorders; balance cortisol levels; build muscle mass, strength and stamina; and boost the immune system.

The following adaptogen herbs are some of the best all-natural options for dealing with stress-related health issues. Even better, they also have other super powers to help you determine which one best fits your unique needs.

Astragalus

There are more than 2,000 species of astragalus, but only two are used medicinally: Astragalus membranaceus and Astragalus mongholicus. Like most adaptogens, astragalus has a long history of use in traditional Chinese medicine and is specifically known for being an immune system booster and disease fighter.

Research even demonstrates how Astragalus membranaceus root supplementation improves immunity while also bolstering antioxidant capacity.

If you're someone who seems to get sick very easily, astragalus may be your best adaptogen option. It's a great choice for anyone trying to boost their immune function and buffer the impact of stress.

Rhodiola

In Tibet, rhodiola (Rhodiola rosea) is a traditional medicine used to increase resistance to physical stress. It also goes by names like "king's crown" and "golden root."

Some studies on animals have linked rhodiola to preventing diet-induced obesity, and since rhodiola helps normalize cortisol levels, it makes sense that it may also help reduce cravings for unhealthy food and discourage the fat accumulation linked to high cortisol levels—specifically fat around the abdomen or belly.

Research has also shown that rhodiola may improve stamina and endurance by increasing red blood cell count and lowering oxidative damage by free radicals.

Rhodiola is a smart choice if you're looking to lower cortisol and encourage healthy weight loss. It may also improve athletic performance and endurance.

Schisandra

In addition, to helping our bodies deal with the negative effects of stress, schisandra is also well known for lowering inflammation and improving liver and digestive function.

The fully ripe, dried berries of the schisandra plants are used to make powder, teas and supplements that can be used medicinally.

Research has shown that these potent berries contain compounds called lignans that seem to actually promote regeneration of damaged liver tissue. Schisandra berries have even been proved to improve cases of chronic viral hepatitis, an inflammatory liver condition.

You should consider schisandra if you want to improve both the health of your liver and your stress response.

Ashwagandha

A pilot study published this year in the Journal of Alternative and Complementary Medicine showed how ashwagandha can help patients with subclinical hypothyroidism. These patients were diagnosed with thyroid disorder but didn't display any obvious symptoms of thyroid deficiency.

Over the course of eight weeks, the treatment group received 600 milligrams of ashwagandha root extract daily, and the control group received starch as a placebo. The researchers found that ashwagandha improved serum thyroid stimulating hormone (TSH) and thyroxine (T4) levels significantly compared to the placebo, revealing the herb's ability to improve hypothyroidism.

This herb is a great option for people who have hypothyroidism in addition to stress and anxiety. Ashwagandha supplementation has also been shown to boost testosterone levels in men who are undergoing infertility screening.

ADAPTOGENS FOR WEIGHT LOSS?

Weight loss can feel like an uphill battle, but research shows that herbal remedies (including adaptogens) can help you reach your weight loss goals faster!

Adaptogens balance hormones

Thyroid hormone deficiency, estrogen dominance, androgen imbalance, insulin resistance, metabolic syndrome, PCOS, cortisol excess – these are just some of the hormone imbalances that contribute to obesity. And unfortunately, losing weight is nearly impossible if your hormones are out of whack. Thankfully, many adaptogens can help. They have been shown to bring the body's hormones back to a healthy balance so you can drop excess weight.

Adaptogens have stress reducing effects

Chronic stress causes an increase in circulating cortisol. Too much cortisol causes the body to hold onto excess belly fat (and keeps you reaching for the cookie jar after a long day's work). By using adaptogens with your weight loss plan, you can reduce the amount of circulating cortisol and the negative effects of stress on your adrenal glands and nervous system.

Adaptogens reduce inflammation

Inflammation and weight gain are closely intertwined. Excess inflammation in the body causes a build-up of swelling and fluids that makes losing weight more difficult. Excess weight only increases inflammation in the body, creating a vicious cycle. With adaptogens, you can naturally reduce inflammation and encourage healthy weight loss.

Adaptogens boost energy

Adaptogens help you feel naturally energized by reducing stress, fatigue, and brain fog.

Adaptogens may reduce cravings

Some studies suggest that adaptogens can help you reduce sugar cravings and control your appetite.

The Best Adaptogenic Herbs for Weight Loss

While many adaptogens help reduce stress and improve overall health, there are some that have a stronger effect on weight loss. Here are a few of the most effective adaptogens you can use to improve your health naturally:

GINSENG VARIETIES (SIBERIAN GINSENG, RHODIOLA ROSEA, AMERICAN GINSENG, CHINESE GINSENG).

One of the world's most famous adaptogens, ginseng is known to increase energy, enhance fat metabolism, and reduce fat absorption. It also helps improve your metabolism and thyroid function.

Natural Herbs for Weight Loss, Energy, and Stress-Relief

1. ASHWAGANDHA

Meaning "smell of a horse," ashwagandha bares a strong aroma and described as "horse-like." But its meaning also serves as a dual purpose, as its has been said its users gain the strength and stamina of a horse!

Ashwagandha is predominately used to manage a number of health conditions, including depression, anxiety, arthritis, insomnia, and diabetes. The adaptogen is also used in hopes to fight against aging, particularly by improving brain function and boosting memory.

2. BACOPA

Customarily used in Indian medicine, bacopa is often acquired to manage pain, anxiety, and overall stress.

Furthermore, there is sufficient evidence suggesting bacopa may be effective in the fight of Alzheimer's disease, as the plant could increase chemicals in the brain involved in memory and thinking.

3. GINSENG

Termed Asian, Chinese, Korean, or American, ginseng tends to take the name of its origin. But despite its birthplace, ginseng is rooted in alternative medicine!

There has been a heavy pool of evidence suggesting the various forms of ginseng are used to manage depression, anxiety, general and chronic fatigue. Ginseng may also improve mental function and protect against Alzheimer's disease and age-related memory loss.

4. MATCHA

Literally meaning "powdered tea," matcha grew its hype as the sippable, green health elixir.

Whereas green tea tea leaves are routinely steeped into hot water then removed, matcha is the literal leaves finely crushed and blended into a solution. (So technically, you are actually drinking the tea leaves.)

And thanks to its potent antioxidants, matcha bares some noteworthy health benefits, including facilitation of fat loss, protection against heart disease, and regulation of blood sugars.

5. TULSI

Touted as the "herb for all reasons" by the Journal of Ayurveda and Integrative Medicine, tulsi has shown to be successful in addressing physical and psychological health conditions.

The adaptogen herb shows to protect organs and tissues against chemical stress from pollutants and heavy metals and physical stress. It has also been found to manage blood glucose, pressure, and lipid levels, along with protecting against depression and problems associated to memory and cognition.

6. RHODIOLA

Trademarked as "artic root," rhodiola is native to the arctic regions of Europe, Asia, and Alaska and has an extensive history as a medicinal plant in Iceland, Sweden, France, Russia, and Greece. Rhodiola is most commonly used for increasing energy, endurance, strength, and mental capacity by helping the body acclimate to and resist physical, chemical, and environmental stressors.

7. SCHISANDRA

Schisandra is often used to combat stress and increase energy, physical performance, and endurance. Furthermore, the adaptogen herb may prevent early aging and promote lifespan.

The adaptogen herb has also shown to be effective in improving liver function in individuals with hepatitis.

CHAPTER FIVE

HEALTHY ADAPTOGEN HERBS, PREPARATION AND FUNCTION

Ashwagandha Recipes:

1. Ashwagandha Golden Milk:

Ingredients:

1 cup almond milk

1/2 teaspoon ashwagandha powder

1/4 teaspoon turmeric

Pinch of black pepper

Honey to taste

Preparation: Heat almond milk with ashwagandha, turmeric, and black pepper. Stir in honey and enjoy.

Function: Calms the nervous system, reduces inflammation, and aids in relaxation.

2. Ashwagandha Berry Smoothie:

Ingredients:

1 cup mixed berries (strawberries, blueberries, raspberries)

1/2 banana

1/2 cup Greek yogurt

1 teaspoon ashwagandha powder

1/2 cup water or almond milk

Preparation: Blend all ingredients until smooth.

Function: Boosts energy, supports the immune system, and provides antioxidants.

3. Ashwagandha Chocolate Energy Bites:

Ingredients:

1 cup rolled oats

1/2 cup almond butter

1/4 cup honey

2 tablespoons cocoa powder

1 teaspoon ashwagandha powder

Preparation: Mix all ingredients, shape into small bites, and refrigerate.

Function: Enhances energy levels, balances stress response, and satisfies cravings.

Rhodiola Recipes:

1. Rhodiola Citrus Iced Tea:

Ingredients:

2 rhodiola tea bags

Juice of 1 orange

Juice of 1 lemon

2 cups water

Honey or maple syrup to taste

Preparation: Brew rhodiola tea, let cool, and mix with citrus juices and sweetener.

Function: Improves mental clarity, boosts mood, and provides refreshing hydration.

2. Rhodiola Breakfast Parfait:

Ingredients:

1 cup Greek yogurt

1/4 cup granola

1 teaspoon rhodiola powder

Mixed berries (blueberries, strawberries)

Chopped nuts (almonds, walnuts)

Preparation: Layer yogurt, granola, berries, and nuts. Sprinkle rhodiola powder on top.

Function: Enhances physical performance, supports cognitive function, and provides protein.

3. Rhodiola Energizing Salad Dressing:

Ingredients:

2 tablespoons olive oil

1 tablespoon lemon juice

1 teaspoon Dijon mustard

1/2 teaspoon rhodiola powder

Salt and pepper to taste

Preparation: Whisk all ingredients together and drizzle over salads.

Function: Increases energy, improves digestion, and adds flavor to salads.

Holy Basil Recipes:

1. Tulsi Green Tea Lemonade:

Ingredients:

2 tulsi tea bags

1 cup green tea, chilled

Juice of 1 lemon

1 tablespoon honey

Preparation: Brew tulsi tea, combine with green tea, lemon juice, and honey.

Function: Supports immune health, provides antioxidants, and quenches thirst.

2. Tulsi Quinoa Salad:

Ingredients:

1 cup cooked quinoa

Chopped cucumber, bell peppers, and red onion

Chopped fresh tulsi leaves

Feta cheese (optional)

Olive oil and lemon juice dressing

Preparation: Combine all ingredients and toss with dressing.

Function: Supports digestion, provides essential nutrients, and adds a refreshing flavor.

3. Tulsi-infused Coconut Water:

Ingredients:

1 cup coconut water

Fresh tulsi leaves

Preparation: Add tulsi leaves to coconut water and let infuse for a few hours.

Function: Hydrates the body, supports electrolyte balance, and provides a natural energy boost.

Eleuthero Recipes:

1. Eleuthero Berry Smoothie Bowl:

Ingredients:

1 frozen banana

1/2 cup mixed berries (blueberries, raspberries)

1/2 cup almond milk

1 teaspoon eleuthero powder

Toppings: granola, sliced banana, chia seeds

Preparation: Blend banana, berries, almond milk, and eleuthero powder. Pour into a bowl and add toppings.

Function: Boosts energy, supports physical performance, and provides antioxidants.

2. Eleuthero Energy Bites:

Ingredients:

1 cup oats

1/2 cup almond butter

1/4 cup honey

1 teaspoon eleuthero powder

Dark chocolate chips (optional)

Preparation: Mix all ingredients, shape into bites, and refrigerate.

Function: Enhances stamina, combats fatigue, and provides a healthy snack.

3. Eleuthero Mushroom Stir-Fry:

Ingredients:

Sliced mixed mushrooms (shiitake, oyster, cremini)

Chopped vegetables (bell peppers, broccoli, carrots)

1 teaspoon eleuthero tincture

Soy sauce or tamari

Preparation: Sauté mushrooms and vegetables, add eleuthero tincture and soy sauce.

Function: Enhances endurance, supports immune health, and adds flavor to dishes.

Schisandra Recipes:

1. Schisandra Berry Elixir:

Ingredients:

1 cup mixed berry juice (cranberry, blueberry, pomegranate)

1 teaspoon schisandra powder

Sparkling water

Preparation: Mix berry juice, schisandra powder, and top with sparkling water.

Function: Supports vitality, promotes skin health, and provides a refreshing drink.

2. Schisandra Chia Seed Pudding:

Ingredients:

2 tablespoons chia seeds

1/2 cup almond milk

1/2 teaspoon schisandra powder

Fresh berries for topping

Preparation: Mix chia seeds, almond milk, and schisandra powder. Let it sit until thickened. Top with berries.

Function: Supports energy, provides omega-3 fatty acids, and enhances digestion.

3. Schisandra Ginger Tea:

Ingredients:

Fresh ginger slices

1 teaspoon schisandra berries (dried)

Honey to taste

Preparation: Steep ginger and schisandra berries in hot water. Add honey.

Function: Boosts immunity, aids digestion, and provides a warming drink.

Ginseng Recipes:

1. Ginseng Breakfast Smoothie:

Ingredients:

1 small apple, chopped

1/2 banana

1/2 cup spinach

1 teaspoon ginseng powder

1/2 cup coconut water

Preparation: Blend all ingredients until smooth.

Function: Boosts energy, supports cognitive function, and provides vitamins.

2. Ginseng Avocado Toast:

Ingredients:

Whole grain toast

Mashed avocado

Sliced tomato

Sprinkle of ginseng powder

Pinch of sea salt and black pepper

Preparation: Spread avocado on toast, add tomato, ginseng powder, and seasonings.

Function: Supports mental clarity, provides healthy fats, and adds a savory breakfast option.

3. Ginseng Iced Herbal Tea:

Ingredients:

2 ginseng tea bags

2 cups water

Lemon slices

Honey to taste

Preparation: Brew ginseng tea, let it cool, add lemon slices and honey, and refrigerate.

Function: Enhances stamina, boosts mood, and provides a refreshing drink.

Maca Recipes:

1. Maca Chocolate Smoothie Bowl:

Ingredients:

1 frozen banana

1 tablespoon cacao powder

1 tablespoon maca powder

1/2 cup almond milk

Toppings: chopped nuts, coconut flakes, cacao nibs

Preparation: Blend banana, cacao powder, maca powder, and almond milk. Top with nuts, coconut, and cacao nibs.

Function: Boosts energy, supports hormonal balance, and provides antioxidants.

2. Maca Breakfast Cookies:

Ingredients:

1 cup rolled oats

1/2 cup mashed banana

1/4 cup almond butter

1 tablespoon honey

1 tablespoon maca powder

Preparation: Mix ingredients, shape into cookies, and bake until golden.

Function: Enhances vitality, supports mood, and provides a nutritious breakfast.

3. Maca Superfood Smoothie:

Ingredients:

1 cup mixed berries (blueberries, raspberries)

1 banana

1 tablespoon hemp seeds

1 tablespoon maca powder

1 cup almond milk

Preparation: Blend all ingredients until smooth.

Function: Supports endurance, provides essential nutrients, and boosts overall well-being.

Astragalus Recipes:

1. Astragalus Immune-Boosting Soup:

Ingredients:

Vegetable broth

Chopped vegetables (carrots, celery, kale)

Sliced mushrooms

1 tablespoon astragalus root slices

Fresh herbs (thyme, rosemary)

Salt and pepper to taste

Preparation: Simmer all ingredients until vegetables are tender.

Function: Supports immune health, provides nutrients, and warms the body.

2. Astragalus Rice Bowl:

Ingredients:

Cooked brown rice

Sautéed mixed vegetables

Sliced grilled chicken or tofu

Drizzle of astragalus-infused olive oil

Preparation: Assemble rice, vegetables, and protein. Drizzle with astragalus-infused oil.

Function: Supports overall wellness, adds flavor to dishes, and provides a balanced meal.

3. Astragalus Herbal Tea Blend:

Ingredients:

1 tablespoon dried astragalus root slices

1 teaspoon dried echinacea

1 teaspoon dried elderberries

Hot water

Preparation: Brew herbs in hot water for a nourishing herbal tea.

Function: Boosts immunity, provides antioxidants, and supports respiratory health.

Licorice Root Recipes:

1. Licorice Root Digestive Elixir:

Ingredients:

1 teaspoon licorice root powder

1/2 teaspoon fennel seeds

1/2 teaspoon ginger powder

Hot water

Preparation: Mix ingredients in hot water for a soothing digestive elixir.

Function: Supports digestion, soothes the stomach, and relieves discomfort.

2. Licorice Root Chai Latte:

Ingredients:

1 cup chai tea

1/4 teaspoon licorice root powder

1/4 teaspoon cinnamon

Honey or maple syrup to taste

Preparation: Mix chai tea, licorice powder, cinnamon, and sweetener.

Function: Enhances energy, adds flavor to beverages, and supports adrenal health.

3. Licorice Root Date Balls:

Ingredients:

1 cup pitted dates

1/2 cup almonds

1 tablespoon licorice root powder

Unsweetened shredded coconut (for rolling)

Preparation: Blend dates, almonds, and licorice powder. Roll into balls and coat with coconut.

Function: Provides sustained energy, satisfies cravings, and supports adrenal function.

Feel free to explore these recipes and adapt them to your taste preferences. As always, if you have any health concerns or are taking medications, it's a good idea to consult with a healthcare professional before incorporating adaptogen herbs into your diet.

CONCLUSION

In conclusion, the world of adaptogen herbs is a fascinating journey into nature's toolbox for promoting balance, resilience, and overall well-being.

Throughout this book, we've delved into the rich tapestry of adaptogens, exploring their historical significance, scientific underpinnings, and myriad potential benefits.

From the calming embrace of Ashwagandha to the invigorating powers of Rhodiola, and the immune-boosting properties of Astragalus, each adaptogen herb offers a unique spectrum of support for the modern challenges of stress, fatigue, and cognitive demands.

As we've uncovered their potential roles in energy enhancement, hormonal balance, and stress management, we've also emphasized the importance of moderation, individualization, and consulting with healthcare professionals.

These ancient allies, hailing from diverse cultures and traditions, have found a place in our contemporary lives as we seek natural solutions for holistic well-being.

Whether you're stirring adaptogens into your morning smoothie, sipping their infused teas, or savoring their unique flavors in culinary creations, their adaptability mirrors their function—helping us adapt to life's ever-changing demands.

As we close this chapter, let us embrace adaptogens not only as herbs but as companions on our journey toward vitality, balance, and the harmonious integration of nature's wisdom into our daily lives.